Englische Übungen

Uwe Kraus
2002 - 2017

© 2022 Uwe Kraus Novivitalis

No.3 Kaiserslautern -

Eselsfürth

Herstellung und Verlag: BoD – Books on Demand, Norderstedt

ISBN: 9783755772859

Über den Autor, über mich- Uwe Kraus

1979, am 17. Februar, wurde ich in Kaiserslautern geboren. Ich machte nach meiner Fachhochschulreife eine Ausbildung zum Maler- und Lackierer an der Meisterschule für Handwerker in Kaiserslautern.

Vor Jahren entdeckte ich die Literatur und Philosophie für mich, die mich zwang zu antworten und zu schreiben.

Neben meinen drei erstveröffentlichten Büchern bei Books on Demand, dem Fußballbuch „Fußball ist unser Leben - Lyrik" 2007, dem Hymnenzyklus "Der Stern des Lebenssinnes" 2001 meinem Frühwerk, und dem Querschnitt meines Denkens, dem "Liebe/gedichte" - Buch erschienen in Zeitschriften für Literatur und Kultur, sowie in Anthologien Gedichte, und zudem ist mein Wirken im Literaturlexikon Rheinlandpfalz festgehalten..

Im April 2009 veröffentlichte ich meine erste Verlagsveröffentlichung "Fernwehpassagen" im Saarbrücker Conte Verlag. Auch 2010 erschien ein Buch im Conte Verlag: "Brainspotting" ist ein lyrisches Roadmovie, das durch meine biographische und irre Schreibweise zu einem modernen Klassiker werden kann...

Im Jahr 2012 kam „Gewichte aus der Zwischenwelt, Wintergedichte, Nachtgedichte" hinzu, die Texte zwischen den Jahren, aus meiner schriftstellerischen Tätigkeit aus dem Zeitraum 2008 – 2012 vereinen. 2003 schrieb ich die Ewu.lution, die apokalyptischen Gedichte, die 2013 bei Bod erschienen. Sie sind ausgestattet mit Bildern des Kaiserslauterer Malers Tony Caulfield und spiegeln, da kurz vor einem Psychiatrieaufenthalt geschrieben, größenwahnsinnige und halluzinogene Inhalte, die auf einer Drogenpsychose in vollem Umfang basieren. 2015 ist ein achtes Buch, durch Telegonos Publishing veröffentlicht worden.. Die Buchstaben, in denen ich schwimme, handeln vom Lieben, Glauben und von meiner Art der Verarbeitung, mittels der ich die vielen gelesenen Eindrücke darstelle und verdichte....

Letzte Veröffentlichungen: „Lichtwechsel" 2016, "Auf dem Weg zurück zu mir" 2017 durch Telegonos Publishing.

 Schriftsteller die ich bewundere und die mich beeinflussten:

George, Heym, Nietzsche, Celan, Ingeborg Bachmann, Novalis, Kafka, Songtexte von Sting, Radiohead, Hermann Hesse, Shakespeare, Lutz Seiler, Rimbaud, Allen Ginsberg, George Byron und Pablo Neruda;

Athlet

drown and out
between the poem titles
of salt and sand
my wisdom will never end

no one follow my stars

arabian languages are completley unable

i evermore fight
with my suburban light

you'll confuse my end
you'll be digging my grave

build me alive

i'm just a child sometimes

empty

like a bullet in my headlights
the overdose
will kill the visions

why i'm explaining my minds

I'll be in deranged action

follow the harvest
and the songs
of guiding brotherhood

don't hide my research

i'm tragic
when i'm over the holding line

my line in my head
will be killed by the barrell

ich bin gekoppelt in dieser
elementaren versdichtung

have a break

in the tiny elementary reflection
i feel fine for the great announce

touch my mouth with silver lips

and feel my sugarplum fingertips

i love to beloved by you
can you answer my revenge

in my emergency
it's my reaction in affection

you're my smile
for a summerwhile

don't demand

I'll be busy and slow
remove me
hold me thrill me kiss me

kill us

you'll be true
my only true love

ende

forever my youngest dead

will watch another step
into heaven
driest weakness will catch my diet

i wanna say don't leave me

you're my frightening healing
of my acid souls

you'll touch me
when i wake up

your kisses smell
like honey wheat

I'am desperate of my
loneliness into your heartache

will you touch my wonderful belongings
i'll never leave you

this my answer:

DU bist mein herz
wenn du bist
bin ich!

temporal

every flight to heaven is
a balance of blame

eternity is a failure
too heavy for the great command

no one ever recalls
i'll be back
in the union of tranquility

and deportation

my wish is like an thundercall

whenever rainbows turn the tides
my mind strikes very lightly

i'm searching for my heart of glass
just to demand
my ambition

to fall into suspicion

i'm the king of weakness
and you're the queen
of my aim...

nobody read the future

depressed echoes

in the hall
angels fall
in the seventh questions of balance
the magic is contained
in a bottle
of whiskey

the soldiers of the tale
made a conduct
of singular permission

my body is swept
under the belief of breakable magic

i ask a question
nobody finds my answer
i'm the pain
i'm the sick
oh honor

i reach till i watch the vision
my ambition

Horrible the captured snake
of the apocalyptic targets
find the reason of demand

help
try to follow
my stairway
unbreakable

UNZERSTÖRBAR DAS HERZBLUT
WILKOMMEN!

level

borrowed the minor sky
in the deep blue
you´ll never walk alone
open your source
with the force of my day

i´ll be back for all time long

ich hatte recht
verstehst du
ich kann keine Gedanken
durch Lichtbrücken fassen

only this is my break
a half time handling

ich werde vor euch stehen
in der Gegenwart vor dem Grab meiner Lüfte
und weinen um Dein Haar Margarethe

Paul Celan gewidmet

zu Todesfuge

Borrowed

My mind explodes in terms of time
I ever recall:
My dreams are captured
In the morning sun

I felt compelled
And narrow of dawn
Insane the power of demand
Is killed in every way

Leave me
Don't leave me any way
Just stairway
The way to fortune's crisis

Elementary the catalysed past
I walk on:
Don't read me between my rhyme
It' s a shame of insanity

do i did

a little bit/
the change of imagination
in my investigation
is traveling in headquarters
of the sublime

my magic is like a non fantastic tragic

I would like to enjoy
the tainted reason of demand

my head explodes in bits of seconds
dreaming of skills of agony

try to arrange my mind
i'm losing my imagination

may the power of light and disagree
is a chapter in my headlights

my borrowed skin is washed
by spies in the stoned elevation

nobody will read my book into my future
it's like a collaborated brick in our rainbows

Words around the subject:

your tuition=

display label
of the heart of glass

forward injection
of investigation

I'm the eye of my spy
do you feel my armageddon

you'll be devised in hearts
and beloved

my love
flown over rainbows

I'm interested in yours
nobody will take this wish

i'm paranoid and destroyed by my agenda
I'll be at

your great services and greetings

I'm happy but crazy

follow the ring in the stonewashed endings of the great wheel in my sky

would you believe

it's dangerous

you'll be my machine in my heart

the motor in the catalysed future

I'm wrapped around your alabaster figure

and my ring is a great answer to all

questions in the moments of every result

why do you ask my questions

I`m drunken and stoned

you'll watch me by my side

don't try to hide

keep my heart alive

Marmelade

Kick the sick
It's obvious

My balanced step
Into eternity
Will call my duty

No one ever is bigger and small
In this burning heartache.

Just you belong
To my search
Of my holy crusade.

I built pictures
Of trades and memories.

Help me I'm refused
My energy is captured
Into heaven and hell-
But my wisdom

Takes care of my business
I'm my and your wish
Across the streets of bluish black
And your submission

Is transmission

Dirty and dust

My explanation isn't a change
I'm searched by my equipment
Of danger

Murderers and faces are passed me by
Thank it's a grendel
A return of the time

The heaven is closed up
Like me too
And a step of the stairways
Is much declared by my mirage
-
This is the place I'll learn to be

Read my book

It's overkill
And confused
The apparition of thunder

Is a room with a view

hello goodbye

this is my offer:

my equality in digital memories.

the contract seems the contact,

it passed me by

it's high time.

hard time to handle with my courage.

only my good old fashioned fantasy.

she's every voice i ever felt.

my salt is my esteem,

my honey is my given she

you're the storm of danger

a liquid glass

like a brilliant I take you to me

but may the heaven is clear blue

like a dove my wish will come through

I died before like a hopeless sinner,

so think about the strongest winner

your luck you'll ever find

like windows and stairways in the clear blue

my morning is a dangerzone

and like a cornerstone

the carnival goes round and round

take this like an energy beam

for my everlasting smile.

I'm a type a ghostwriter an entertainer and a big bastard:

wouldn't you miss me?

I like you too

© Uwe Kraus KL, den 08.09.2016

the program

are any men dying in the cast of senses
is my exploded happiness a brutal past tense
noone is evermore
in the battle of done before
i reput the program of my b
i'm programmable
with grammar
and my minds an inclusion
of a step into the distance

i found you in my dirt
and you're older than i
in my eye the spy
who loves the darkness like a beauty

bloody sweat
an monster of organizing
an wish of my paradises

any fact:

in the factory my mind smokes
for the rhyme of my blues

i'm a signal
a roboter of words
an machine who turns our tides
into majesty and honey

(C) Uwe Kraus 13.11.2016

r.e.m.

Follow the wind
Follow the stars
Into the weaping of a claw of suggestion
I'm buried the major in marriage
And drawing weakness

You'll stay awake
In my window an colour of light
My power is knowledge of unknown
My claim is such a shame
Wonder the wonderer

I'm I into the lying of love
Open your smell eyed rapid moves
My believe my sweat my teardrop
You'll be

© Uwe Kraus 24.11.2016

Wear my eyes behind

From the moments of unending feelings
To sharing the highest decease
I count seconds in parts of hours
And fly to parts between
My blind eyes
To close the lines
And walk behind

I wear my eyes infront of my neck
Close and deep in mind
I fall to watch the towers out of heavens signs
The eyes closer and the feelings grow to
Sleep into the miracles of dawn.
My friend is gone
Is gone

Dawn and endlessly the inside out
Behind from me
Is dark and waves from the
Sea are sounding and surround my agony.

Where the blinds and helpless end
The truth and breaks are ending now
To wear the inside out

God get off with the rain out of my brain

Do you think i´m closer
When you treat me older
And my feelings are lower
Do you think my nervous snakes behind my eyes
Will shut to the youngest lies.

I feel you mean to tell me that mirrors
Remember faces growing to the wall
And get my wishes all in all
To blind the magic
In all non fantastic tragic.

You mean to tell me that songs we sing
Come strange and deranged
Throughout my kind
So take my brain outside the guiding lines
And get off with the rain out of my mind.

Refrain:

It´s all i see that songs remains the same to me.
Why do you laugh infront of my dreaming skills
To ring the bells that never are in my visions
All together that's division!

Do you

Do you see the mirror in the skies
That fading sunset in the deep blue
That questioning about?
Do you mean that maniacs
Come out in front of feels.

Is this the love that my soul is sharing for
In dynamic contracts we give to me
Are you disappearing
Behind my smile
When the sun is brighter in my sign..

Would you climb the highest waves
Through minor and major skies
That are flowing with a breeze behind the wolves
Of waterlines and wear the hair
Into my face and kiss the blood of waterman?

Refrain:

Where the home is
And where the love spills
And where the blood flows
That's gonna be the highest rise
Just take these lines and fading through my mind...

When the sunset kills the beast..

For a while step by step
I thought so bravely and whole to show
My pieces of construction
Of pain and interruption
To feel to do to make the game in shame
My name
Who stops the rain?

When fires are burning through the nights
I find my word
I'm searching day by day
The number of the way the way
To be and in my shields of watereyes
The beasts are blowing time by time

The sun has killed the beast
The feelings and meanings
Of being powerful and strange
To calm the smoke
Of cigarettes i breath the air
And go to wear the word behind my doing
To take a trip and dream the technical
Dreams of being elementary metaphysical.

Refrain:

When the whole has holed the heavens
I step beside to hide
The words are gone a new way has come: maroon

The fire ending here you know

When words are spoken
Bones are broken and
The fire killed the west
And east of light and disagreement
Is still the heart an
Thunderball which shares a visual galaxy.

You know things are strange in minds when
Signs are postcards
And meanings are explosions
Stars can burn and
Feelings can learn
At the coasts of young and old.

I got fireworks and pistols
To make my imagination despair
Of brain-end and coast of silver land
I got a book for every flight to heaven
And a look for every kind of permission.
That's all: the fire ending here you know?

Refrain:

The fires ending in the shine of light
The fight is ending by the might
Of right and disillusion: you know?

Wonderful enigma

Why is the past is travelling in
Terms of time
Relativity is a game
Why we live the synchronization
With the members who
Crawl laws
And gave steel to the poison in time when dynamite
Exploded in our heads of crime.

Who gave the questions to the answers
Who gave the crime to the sublime
In lines of shining
Paradises in the waves of time:
Who do you think you be when
Songs surround the feels
Of faith and majority
In having parts of powder
Which explode like atoms in the garden of hiroshima?

Refrain:

We love to kill and thrill the parts of time
In the shape of lines
Who brought the bombs to man
And feels the love that never ends?

The grass are flowing through the love of a silhouette

Black covers of magazines are piling up
Beside my bed and
Things get amazing when you fall
Off steps of stairways.
I build with the love of my cigarettes
A burning heart and
Smell the taste of slippering ways
Beyond the front of people's voices
Who calm breath into my choices.

When grass was green and shadows
Falling small and high to calling
You know the silhouettes are loving
My choice of drawing in the smoke
And light the pipe is high
And closer to travelling the most of famous
Ways to lay beside and
Dream of the other side!

Refrain:

The grass are green and taste is high
And famous things are passing by.
The shadows follow loveliness
The green heart that's the way to be
I feel the growing harmony!

When dynamic closes feelings

Do yá feel the light
Which shines brightly out of that heroes eyes?
And see the wind will fall to every street
To cities behind the capitol of lock
Tick tock
When clocks began to stand still and
Will to will will fall
Into famous halls
You know then the dynamic closes feelings
And shows meanings between walls
And materials

Martyrs are blinding buildings in streets of
Danger with no tower in heroes dreams
The fall of heaven is a call
To ride between line after line
Between death and solution
Some kind of confusion.
He turns the watches and gives
The men policy he spelled the second
Dynamic closes
Wishes:
See what the truth means to relativity!

Sometimes love can build up towers and defeat them in two hours

When the rain climbs through snakes
In a wave beyond the melting
You see hearts can build towers
And some kind of bad can destroy feelings within hours.
The truth is love always
The parts of melting hearts
And of boiling points around your spinning wheels.

When love turns tables
And your friends are able to
Construct a conduct of
Harmony beyond her smiles
Songs always climb
Through mountains
When you find your signs.

Refrain:

Sometimes loves grower
In things lower
Closer
Or far away
A cry
To lie
A meaning to be
In perfect kinds of feelings

Ende:

Thank you for listening to me
It´s just a controversial view
Of points of me
And you!

Follow the stars (far to andromeda)   David Bowie gewidmet

With the masters in the sky
I share my eyes for contracts
While my wishes contact
The mind
In the shuttle we raised down and out of
The world aloud
To couple every space beyond the time
And reached a fading line
Over bridges out of
Universes into nova space
And grow lower the engines outside of mine
Will closer into my water mark
When commanders told me to wake up from
Holes faded black
And magnets taking out the symbols
Of evolution and minor light
Crawls the error
We faded galaxy to mirror world
Of being exactly in the magenta legends
The fall and the end
Of story will soon be told:
We reached a second moon
Once large we became small
Once big we became little
And only magenta
Was it mental-
Or liquid groundcontrol?
We want to break the spheres
And then we get closer to the tunneltime:
Wake up
The dream is over
Magenta:
Only andromeda!

If only (are you lonely)

See me walking through the doors
Behind your eyes
And build up rackets in great winterskies
You watch from towers out of heavens gates to
See the frame to send my name
Insanely you said to me watch the waves only lonely by the sea
Don´t ask me for more instead
My bed
Is cold and feelings are growing passionately to see
What goes comes and goes
What walls crawl into the heavens lies
We want to grow beside to hide
I do what i want and feel what i lend to spend
Inside the wonders
Don´t you see that's the end
Of no romance?
 I want to cry out in symbols and calm my breath from shaking
Cigarettes on the lips to dry
Soul can be folded up when things close
And flowers grow
We lie and lie
And why can't you see
We belong to
you and me?

A little girl with wavy eyes

Would you lie
If i asked would you be
Mine after a great reward and spaces that shake from emptiness to
eternity
Then close my lips with fingertips and sleep beside my
Arms and climb my shadows from smiles you give
Can´t it be forgiven what i felt the days after
You leaving and my wisps of health in winterair they told me you´ll
be there
With wavy eyes miles of hours i pretend
Your hand would be gone
And mine when things close and roses rise through parts of billion
bites between the shattering eyes i
give to you in splattered ways my heart was broken and words of
love will be spoken when i look into your eyes
now, come on tell me no lies
with rackets that cracked beyond the universes that's my figure
with injured motions
like me we
can be or can´t we tell this by unspoken melody
from metaphors of metal my heat is stopped from raising blood into
the organs just a moment my head explodes from thin ice when
you're close i think it´s better to be given things in parts of
whispering breezes you rain down in a kind of strange feeling

Refrain:

a little girl with wavy blue eyes
Is sent from angel skies
attract the looks beyond horizons
climbs in moviescenes
with French subtitles
that's a kiss of blood and feelings of god.

blue pills

dread the smell
of the pills

busy and slow my emotion.
dreaming of skills of agony-

why i should take this crystal bag
in my sound

no one reads my book of my future
and takes the paper monster's stairways

i´ve found my melody
and it sound like ebony-
don´t take me away

into the dark side of morrow

Vater

Lost in trance
The tides between
I feel in eruption
And patiently my agony
Will swim into my fantasy-

Let me be in danger

Every time is quick
Just quick to be innocent
And quiet-.

Or is time to handle
With my courage

I´ve taken the overdose
Just to be in a trace

But mellow is dread
To construct the conduct

Paralysed

Every brick over the rainbows
Collaborated with my evolution
No one can touch my visions
Into the dark rise of evil

Just only the click of my tale
Is some reason of demand

Horrible and quick just the kick of my emotion

The earth will calm my breath

Fortune is a crisis
Only love can kill this

You will be loved by the power
Of my strength
And hold my damaged sign

Into this waterline

Uwe Kraus Birkenfeld, den 13.07.2015

Borrow

Tomorrow my sorrow
Will kill the west and east
Of light and disagreement

My book is like an candle
In my hand
You´ll watch me by

I fridge the freeze
And morrow my capital
Is my first lock

Do you realize
Or try to understand

I will always love you

Buffalo

The quiet perfect pitch isn´t
Anything to gamble with
Like million dollars

don´t fly high
Over prison cells
The tainted game is dead

Forever baby smile
And don´t pull on to cry

Buy universes supernovas
Hellfired bones and try
To fall out in heavens eyes

You´ll everytime be my maid
I´ll love you

Praise you

Power of grayskull is a
Magic chapter in my ambition

The childhood is ending here..

Answer the question
You´ll take my words out of my mouth

Dangerzone increased
The yellow bag of sand
In my attempt

Will you follow their way

Will you be there in action
In a deranged atmosphere

Old whispering birds take
The rise to hell
And wait for their time in prison cells

Ich stehle die begegnung
In faktum mortu megadeath

Ich werde folgen dir wohin du auch gehst:
Bis ans ende des kindseins

Doch weiß ich ich bin nicht allein
Die zeit läuft für uns
Im prägnanten moment...

Ich halte den stift waagrecht:
Es ist mitternacht...

& du wirst folgen mir
Wenn du nicht wohlweislich
Mein ende beschreitest

Crazy

Come on touch me
Inside my boiling soul
The reason for liquid answers in my brain

I felt compelled and nasty of narrowness
Nobody knows the papermonsters
Where I want to be

Come on suck in the chips of my damaged brain

I´ll hope you be in the office too

cat

scratch me back
into difficult memory
inside the breakable freedom
arrange me
my levee
I'm connected with the blue
swept water
my signal is an act
to scroll around the pictures
of my revenge

you'll watch me at my side
into my closed elevated summer

a morning will not come again

again. will she offer her
tongue's
torch advertize me conjugate me
for purple division

into my equality

Abschied an den Leser

Wenn du von allem dem, was diese Blätter füllt,
Mein Leser, nichts des Dankes wert gefunden:
So sei mir wenigstens für das verbunden,
Was ich zurück behielt.

(Gotthold Ephraim Lessing)

Weitere Bücher des Autors:

Der Stern des Lebenssinnes . 2001 . Gedichte, Hymnen . Bod

Fußball ist unser Leben . 2007 . Lyrik . Bod

Liebe/gedichte Lyrik aus neun Jahren . 2008 . Bod

Fernwehpassagen . 2009 . Gedichte . Conte Verlag

Brainspotting . Erzählung . 2010 . Conte Verlag

Gewichte aus der Zwischenwelt . 2012 . Bod

Ewu.lution – Apokalyptische Gedichte . 2013 . Bod

Die Buchstaben, in denen ich schwimme . 2016 . Telegonos

Lunatics 2014 . Bod

Lichtwechsel . Gedichte . 2016 . Telegonos

Auf dem Weg zurück zu mir . 2017 . Telegonos